THE EMPIRE STATE BUILDING
AND MANHATTAN
SKYSCRAPERS

BONECHI

Introduction

New York is famous throughout the world for the tall buildings that characterize its skyline. Day or night the contours of its famous towers bid a breathtaking welcome to Manhattan: the "pencil point" of the Empire State Building, the curving Art Déco top of the Chrysler Building and, until September 11, 2001, the two parallelepipeds of the Twin Towers that stood out against the sky even miles and miles away from the heart of New York City.

And the effect is even stronger when you look at the city from the top of these buildings: the grid of streets, tiny cars that seem to scamper about and a horizon that extends literally as far as the eye can see is an astonishing experience to say the least. And, as one of the early visitors to the Empire State Building said, "first you are dumbstruck and immobile and then you

gradually become aware of how spectacular it all is." A "skyscraper" was the triangular skysail on a clipper ship, but by the end of the 19th century it was attributed to tall the buildings which began to appear alongside of the masts of the ships anchored in New York harbor.

Not only are skyscrapers the greatest tourist attraction in the Big Apple, they are also this city's greatest contribution to the history of architecture. In just a few square miles you can cover a fascinating itinerary that will take you from the late 19th century to our day and observe a variety of styles ranging from the Neo-Gothic Woolworth Building to the deconstructivism of the new Condé Nast Building. Less obvious but of fundamental importance are the engineering innovations developed by the architects and builders: from the invention of the

The Empire State Building is the undisputed protagonist of New York's skyline.

elevator to the creation of the metallic bearing infrastructures. The "spell" of the skyscraper is definitely in the audacious combination of all these elements that comprise one of the most visible tributes to human ingenuity in the 20th century. The Empire State Building is the New Yorkers' favorite skyscraper even though its record as the world's tallest building was broken decades ago. Along with the Statue of Liberty it is the unmistakable symbol of the world's greatest metropolis.

The lights of the Empire State Building dominate the nighttime skyline.

On pages 10-11: an aerial view of Manhattan stretching to Central Park, in the background on the left.

STYLE	PERIOD	FEATURES	ARCHITECTS	BUILDINGS
Beaux Arts	1885-1920	Revival of styles from the past: classic, Gothic, Renaissance	C. Gilbert, D. Burnham, McKim, Meade & White	Flatiron, Woolworth Building
Art Déco	1920-1940	Symmetry, aerodynamic lines inspired by industrial design	R. Hood, Shreve, Lamb & Harmon, W. Van Alen	Chrysler Building, Empire State Building, Rockefeller Center, Radio City Music Hall
International Style	1930-1970	Functionalism, modernism, pure lines, essential design	W. Gropius, Le Corbusier, L. Mies van der Rohe	Met-Life, World Trade Center, United Nations Headquarters
Postmodernism	1980-today	Eclecticism, individualism, incorporation of touches of past styles, playfulness	R. Meler, M. Graves, R.A.M. Stern	Trump Tower, Condé Nast Building, The Lipstick

ESB: where it is

The Empire State Building stands in the heart of Manhattan, on Fifth Avenue between 33rd and 34th Streets.

Located between 33rd and 34th Streets, between Broadway and Fifth Avenue, the Empire State Building is in the heart of New York's business district. Extending over an area of nearly 79,000 square feet (7340 square meters) it covers the entire block. The address, 350 Fifth Avenue was famous even before this masterpiece of modern architecture was erected. It was the site of the Waldorf Astoria, the hotel that made an era as the meeting place for society, politicians and businessmen. In the Thirties the hotel moved to its current Park Avenue address. And before that it was the home of Caroline Schermerhorn Astor whose "Four Hundred Ball" was the highlight of the New York social calendar during the *Belle Époque*. Nearby is Macy's, built in 1902, the internationally famed store that is still operating the world's first escalator that is built entirely from wood. The other nearby attractions are Madison Square Garden (32nd Street and 7th Avenue) the famous sports arena, the Church of St. John the Baptist (34th Street and Broadway) with the magnificent tabernacle by Napoleon Le Brun and the General Post Office (33rd Street and 8th Avenue) one of the finest examples of neoclassical – known as Beaux Arts – architecture the city has to offer that is open 24 hours a day.

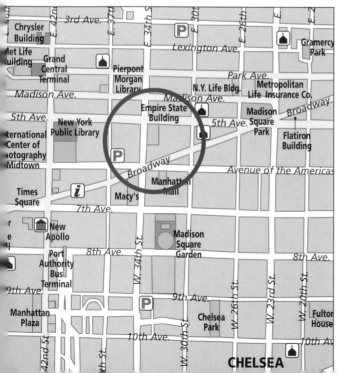

Opposite, box, a late nineteenth century photo of Fifth Avenue looking north, with a bit of Central Park in the background.

Architecture in New York

*In 1950 an **antenna**, used for radio broadcasts, was added to the **tower**, bringing the total height of the Empire State Building to 1,454 feet (443,2meters).*

***Pyramidal structures** made it possible to build tall buildings that would not block off light from surrounding buildings and to eliminate strong winds that would have been generated at street level.*

In New York you can see every style of architecture that has come into vogue since the 19th century to the present. In fact, this city has the world's largest variety of skyscrapers. The first buildings of this type appeared on the skyline in the late 19th century, the years of New York's first business and industrial boom. That period also marks the beginning of a series of determinant technological innovations such as the invention of the elevator, industrial steel making and the development of fire-proof materials.

The 13-story Tower Building that was opened in 1888 is considered the first skyscraper ever raised in New York. In architectural terms these early buildings were inspired by styles of the past such as Neo-Gothic or neoclassical. The finest examples from this period are the Flatiron Building and the monumental Woolworth Building that contemporaries nicknamed the "cathedral of commerce". Soon the people realized that the skyscrapers were blocking out considerable amounts of light from the nearby buildings and were creating strong air currents on the streets below. For this reason in 1916 New York passed zoning regulations that forced builders to decrease the constructed surface area as the buildings rose in height, and this led to the advent of the pyramid skyscraper. Starting in the Twenties, Art Déco and the Bauhaus made themselves felt to the point of giving rise to two outstanding structures: the Chrysler Building and the Empire State Building. The modernist style gained strength during the following decade to flourish after World War II with the International movement. The linear shapes and motifs along with the use of glass curtain walls distinguish the buildings of this period that include the United Nations Building, the Twin Towers of the World Trade Center and the Pan Am building. Postmodernism came onto the scene in the Eighties, and in architecture this led to the neo-modernist and deconstructivist movement.

Here Comes the Elevator

Skyscrapers could not exist if someone had not invented the elevator. The first steam-powered elevator was developed by Elisha Otis in 1852. Five years later the E.G. Otis company installed the first commercial, passenger elevator in a New York department store. By 1873 there were over 2000 elevators operating in the United States. In the coming years Otis developed the hydraulic elevator that was less expensive and more efficient than the steam powered version. 1889 was the year of the first electric elevator that became semi-automatic in 1924 stopping at the requested floors without need for an operator.

The fully automatic elevator came into being in 1948, while in 1982, thanks to variable frequency technology, acceleration and stopping became more gradual.

The latest innovation came in 1996 with the revolutionary Odyssey system that permits both vertical and horizontal movement so that the cabs can occupy the same shaft, opening the doors to a new generation of elevators.

*A perspective shot of the **Empire State Building** and the spire of the **Marble Collegiate Church** that dates from 1854. In the box, the original interior of one of the **skyscraper's elevators**.*

By reacting to what had become a banal style architects designed original buildings that reinterpreted and combined motifs from previous eras. The Trump Tower is one example: the use of glass and straight lines recall the International style, but the original diagonal, staggered perimeters are a distinctive feature of contemporary decorativist architecture.

Zoom on the Empire

Even though its more than forty-year "title" as the world's tallest building was broken in 1972, the Empire State Building still holds some impressive – and unsurpassed – records. From the artistic standpoint, it was the first American skyscraper to assimilate the lesson of the modernist school that had been launched in Europe by the Bauhaus. The simplicity of design and the harmony of its various elements confer still unsurpassed subdued elegance. The recesses on the façades, for example, not only augment the dramatic effects of shadow and depth, they also increase the number of corner offices that are preferred because they have better lighting. The Empire State Building was also the first building to have visible, chrome-plated metal risers that serve both structural and decorative purposes, emphasizing the vertical grace. This technique, that permitted a marked reduction in the structure's specific weight, is considered a revolutionary architectural innovation.

Even the interior design was marked by several significant "novelties" such as the use of semi-permanent dividing walls that made it possible to offer tenants custom-sized offices; placing the radiators below the windows in the niches created by the sills, saving space and

A 204 feet television antenna was erected in 1950.

The soaring tower was developed to anchor dirigibles.

The observation decks are famous for the amazing view of the city.
Ever since it was built, the observation decks have been the secret of the building's fame and fortune, as they draw an endless stream of visitors. Actually, the original plans only called for one observation deck on the 86th floor that was to be the top of the building. When the tower was added, another was created on the 102nd floor.

The exterior surface of the skyscraper is dotted by 6,500 windows.
An impressive number that gives the Empire State Building a particularly luminous face, a face that becomes even more luminous and impressive when the colored spotlights on the top thirty stories are lit. There is a specific color for each holiday and celebration.

The Empire State Building has 73 elevators and they travel at top speed.
Passenger and freight elevators travel 1312 feet (400 meters) per minute and are indispensable to the daily life of the Empire State Building.

concealing them at the same time; and finally, the central position of the elevator shaft made available the maximum of usable floor space. From the engineering standpoint this skyscraper was the first building ever erected from prefabricated, standard-size components such as beams, pillars and windows that were assembled on site. It was this system that made it possible to put up the building in record time: about four and a half stories per week! Work was organized with maximum efficiency, it was an assembly line operation. A rail transport system was built on each floor to distribute materials quickly and with a minimum effort: the trucks were unloaded in the basement, directly onto the elevators that carried the supplies to their destination.

Construction was a real show for New Yorkers. Every day a fascinated crowd would gather to watch the extraordinary, bustling progress of the works and mainly the breathtaking acrobatics of the workers suspended hundreds of feet above ground.

Lewis Hines' famous photographs document this event that was epoch-making for the city and its people. The work of over 3000 men was coordinated with utmost precision and the contractors were selected for the quality of their products and their ability to meet deadlines. It was thanks to this efficient logistical organization that the Empire State Building could be completed in one year and 45 days, one month ahead of schedule. Therefore, the Empire State Building can justly be considered a masterpiece of beauty and efficiency.

The use of prefabricated components made it possible to erect the Empire State Building in record time.

The skyscraper grew at the dizzying rate of four stories a week. The facing was brick, while the windows were framed with steel panels; steel was also the material used for the decorative elements.

*1930: **workers at dizzying heights** positioning a heavy slab during **construction** of the Empire State Building.*

© Collection of The New-York Historical Society (Negative Number 67435)

Technical Notes

Entrances: 5 on 33rd St., 5th Ave. and 34th St.
Total height: 1,454 feet (443.2 meters)
Antenna height: 204 feet (62 meters)
Floors: 102
Steps: 1860
Windows: 6500
Occupied floor space:
Area of site 79,288 square feet (7,340 square meters)
Weight: 365,000 tons

Weight of steel reinforcements: 60,000 tons (completed in 23 weeks)
Foundation supports: 200 steel and cement pylons
Facing: 10 million bricks
Foundation depth: 525 feet (16.7 meters)
Elevators: 73 (able to travel 1,181 feet/360 meters per minute)
Observatories: 2 (86th and 102nd floors)
Maintenance staff: 150

The Observation Decks

After the spire of the Chrysler Building was unveiled as a surprise upon the completion of construction, to reach a height of 1046 feet (319 meters), the Empire State Building would have only been 26 inches (66 centimeters) taller according to the original plans. And that was certainly too little for the ambitions of Raskob and Smith. On 11 December 1929 Al Smith announced the construction of a 200 feet (60,8 meters) tower that would not be merely decorative as the one on the Chrysler building, but looking to the future, would have a specific, practical purpose. The tower was conceived as a mooring for transatlantic dirigibles. This modification radically changed all the plans for the top of the Empire State Building that was to have been 85 stories high with a flat roof. A story, with huge windows was added (the 86th floor observation deck) as was a tower that included a waiting room for passengers going to the 101st floor, and a platform for dirigible mooring on the next story.

Every year more than 3.5 million people visit the 86th floor observation deck. Situated 1050 feet (320 meters) above ground, this area consists of a terrace and an indoor area with souvenir shops and a fast-food bar.

The outdoor terrace runs along the entire perimeter of the building and powerful Bausch & Lomb telescopes make it possible to view the magnificent panorama of New York and its surroundings.

The 86th floor observation deck offers a spectacular view of the whole city.

The Tower and the Dirigibles

In the Twenties, dirigibles were considered to be the future of long-distance transportation. However, they presented considerable problems for landing in cities since some of them were over 1000 feet (300 meters) long and needed considerable space for maneuvering. According to Al Smith, the Empire State Building offered the ideal solution to the problem: the dirigibles could have landed on top of the building.

This was the impetus for the construction of the tower with a mooring platform on the 102nd floor where passengers could disembark along a walkway...spine chilling to say the least.

After refueling and embarking passengers for the next trip the dirigible could take off. The aeronautical engineers were skeptical from the start because of the strong winds which at that height would have made mooring very difficult. In spite of this Al Smith did not give up and ran a series of tests that proved the experts correct. The idea was quickly and quietly abandoned and the passenger waiting room was transformed into the observatory that was open to the public.

Facing page: a 1931 photo of the Empire State Building, the building was complete except for the tower that was to be a mooring for dirigibles.

Originally there was only a masonry parapet, but a protective fence was added later to discourage suicide attempts. In the Thirties and Forties the Empire State Building café-restaurant was a rather elegant rendezvous: tearoom during the day and a sophisticated cocktail lounge in the evening. But as the years went by, and with remodeling they have lost all their original charm and character.

In the early Eighties what was the waiting room for dirigible passengers was converted into the circular observatory on the 101st floor which is commonly considered the 102nd because this was the level that was supposed to have been the mooring platform and observatory, but it was considered too small and too dangerous to open to the public. Today the observatory on the "102nd" floor is closed due to the limited space and the long waiting lines that formed. Now it is only opened for special events. In any case, a visit to the Empire State Building, even if you can only go to the 86th floor is still an unforgettable experience. Thanks to its position in the heart of Manhattan, day and night (it is open until midnight) the terrace offers a view of the entire city, with the bridges that connect Manhattan to the other boroughs and the spectacular tops of the surrounding skyscrapers such as the Chrysler Building.

Cocktails at 86

The Empire State Building bar-restaurant with its magnificent view of the East River and Long Island is located on the east side of the 86th floor observatory.
Initially it was an elegant rendezvous to have a cocktail and admire a magnificent sunset or the city lights. The bar was made of fine Belgian marble, comfortable rattan chairs were grouped around the tables, and there were five different types of champagne. "Enjoy the pleasure of a cocktail in a plane without ever leaving the ground" said an advertisement of the period. A Martini – ever the New Yorkers' favorite – cost 25 cents, but Manhattan, the Bronx and, of course Empire State, cocktails were popular among the customers of the world's highest bar. The style has changed several times since then and now it is not very different from what you can find at other tourist attractions throughout the United States.

Lights and Colors

Manhattan nights are brightened by the colored lights on the top thirty stories of the Empire State Building.

The Empire State Building has a formidable lighting system that creates a fascinating spectacle on New York's nighttime skyline. The top was first illuminated in 1932 with a beacon to celebrate Franklin D. Roosevelt's election as President of the United States (he had been governor of New York State). The building was blacked out during World War II, but in 1956 it once again shined in the New York sky with the "Freedom Lights", five enormous revolving beacons that symbolized a "welcome to the land of liberty in the air age", and which, under ideal weather conditions were visible as far as Boston. In 1964 on the occasion of the New York World's Fair, the beacons were replaced by fixed white lamps that drenched the entire façade in light. 1976 marked the beginning of the use of colored lights when the Yankees once again won the World Series. The following year the Empire State Building lights were colored to commemorate the most important events, celebrations and seasons of the year: red and green during the Christmas holidays, white and blue for United Nations Day, red white and green for Columbus Day.

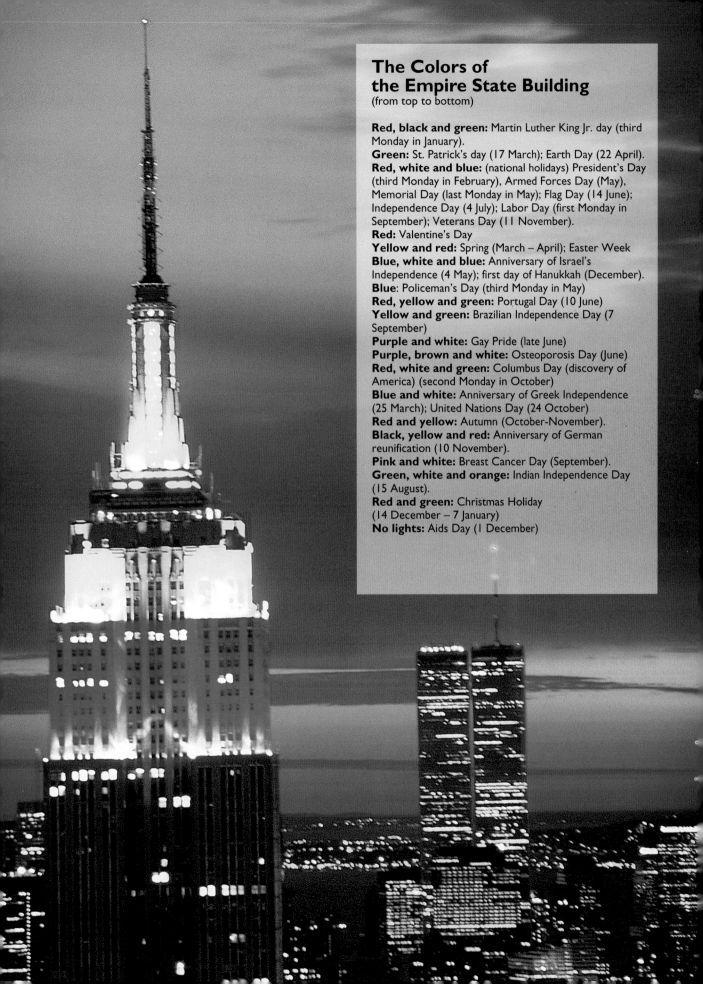

The Colors of the Empire State Building
(from top to bottom)

Red, black and green: Martin Luther King Jr. day (third Monday in January).
Green: St. Patrick's day (17 March); Earth Day (22 April).
Red, white and blue: (national holidays) President's Day (third Monday in February), Armed Forces Day (May), Memorial Day (last Monday in May); Flag Day (14 June); Independence Day (4 July); Labor Day (first Monday in September); Veterans Day (11 November).
Red: Valentine's Day
Yellow and red: Spring (March – April); Easter Week
Blue, white and blue: Anniversary of Israel's Independence (4 May); first day of Hanukkah (December).
Blue: Policeman's Day (third Monday in May)
Red, yellow and green: Portugal Day (10 June)
Yellow and green: Brazilian Independence Day (7 September)
Purple and white: Gay Pride (late June)
Purple, brown and white: Osteoporosis Day (June)
Red, white and green: Columbus Day (discovery of America) (second Monday in October)
Blue and white: Anniversary of Greek Independence (25 March); United Nations Day (24 October)
Red and yellow: Autumn (October-November).
Black, yellow and red: Anniversary of German reunification (10 November).
Pink and white: Breast Cancer Day (September).
Green, white and orange: Indian Independence Day (15 August).
Red and green: Christmas Holiday (14 December – 7 January)
No lights: Aids Day (1 December)

THE ORIGINS AND HISTORY OF THE EMPIRE STATE BUILDING

The Fifth Avenue and 34th Street around 1880, the site where the world's largest hotel, the Waldorf Astoria was built in 1897. The hotel was torn down to make room for the Empire State Building.

The Empire State Building's Sponsors

John Raskob was born in Lockport New York in 1879. He began his career as a bookkeeper at Du Pont and thanks to his business sense, he soon became personal assistant to the chairman, Pierre S. Du Pont. After World I, Raskob suggested investing in General Motors that had been in financial trouble for years. With a 50 million dollar investment Du Pont became the majority shareholder in GM and appointed Raskob Vice-President and chief financial officer. In 1919 Raskob invented the installment payment plan that immediately made the automobile available to nearly everyone. Just eight years later, 60% of the cars on American roads had been purchased on the installment plan. During that same period Raskob began to sympathize with the anti-prohibition movement which, in his opinion infringed on civil liberties, he became its spokesman and got to know Alfred E. Smith and the Democratic Party. In 1928 Al Smith appointed him chairman of the National Committee and manager of his campaign for the Presidency of the United States.

Alfred E. Smith was born in Brooklyn in 1873 to an Irish family. He began working odd jobs at a very young age: dockworker at the fish market, truck driver and plumbing supply salesman. The turning point in his life came in 1895 when he was offered a job as a marshal. He entered politics in 1903 when he ran – and was elected – to the New York State Assembly. After a tragic fire in 1911 he came into the limelight as a defender of workers' rights, and seven years later his popularity won him the governorship of New York State. Alfred E. Smith was certainly one of the most visible, and well-loved personalities of his time with his dark brown derby, a formidable memory and an ability to invent historic metaphors. Ten years later he ran for the presidency of the United States and lost. The following year, together with John Raskob he announced the construction of the Empire State Building; he was chairman and the personification of the project until his death in 1944.

Al Smith (right) and Winston Churchill, just one of the many famous people who have visited the Empire State Building.

Thanks to outstanding economic growth during the Twenties, construction was a sound investment – especially in New York. With the advent of the skyscraper and the new method of building upwards, the city's skyline was destined to change forever.

Right: a Deluxe "Model A" Ford Roadster, vintage 1930.

E ven today the Empire State Building is a seductive symbol of New York all over the world. But this building, that was erected between 1930 and 1931 is also the culmination of an historically important period for the city. During the economic boom of the "roaring Twenties" the skyscraper became the preferred symbol of prestige and power among the new captains of industry. This triggered a race to the sky that would change the city's appearance forever.

According to history, the idea for the Empire State Building was born during a survey. John Raskob, president of General Motors and main backer of the corporation took a pencil in hand and told the architect who was with him "It has to look like this." The design work was assigned to Shreve, Lamb & Harmon who completed the work that had already been started, designing the upper stories as construction progressed. Another key figure was Alfred E. Smith, former governor of New York State, who contributed with his popularity not only to promoting this historic building, but also helping it to survive the Great Depression of the nineteen Thirties.

During the third decade of the century, the United States was enjoying a period of such extraordinary economic growth that the era was dubbed "the roaring Twenties." New York, in particular was in a strategic position to take advantage of these favorable circumstances, to become - thanks to the best commercial harbor on the Atlantic coast of the U.S.- the main junction for trade with Europe and the eastern United States. At the time real estate and construction were considered excellent investments, especially in New York where growth seemed unstoppable. The residential areas spread horizontally, expanding the city's boundaries towards the suburbs, while the vertical growth of the downtown business districts was about to change the city's skyline. In 1929 there were already 188 skyscrapers in New York. By the end of the Twenties, the first signs of market saturation began to be felt: the supply of business space definitely exceeded the demand. In spite of all this, the idea for the Empire State Building – a child of Al Smith – was born during spring of 1929. Both promoters of the project, Al Smith and John Raskob, like the majority of the period's skyscraper builders did not have any

The

1929: the Stock Market Crash and the End of the "Roaring Twenties"

October 29, 1929 has gone down in history as the official beginning of the Great Depression, the profound economic crisis that enveloped the United States and the entire world during the Thirties. On that day Wall Street lost between 10 and 15 billion dollars, causing panic throughout the country. The unbridled optimism of the Twenties and some permanent effects of World War I had caused major market imbalances that had to be adjusted. The crisis reached its nadir in 1933 when more than 15 million Americans, a fourth of the labor force, were unemployed and about 40% of all American banks had failed. The economy began to revive in the late Thirties thanks to the "New Deal" launched by President Franklin Delano Roosevelt.

experience in the construction business. The former was a politician and the latter a businessman. Their partnership, based on their common humble Irish-Catholic origins and great success in their respective professions had been ongoing for years. After Alfred E. Smith's defeat in the presidential race of 1928, they still wanted to do something great together, and the tallest building in the world seemed ideal. On 29 August 1929 they announced their plans to the public. The architects they chose were Shreve, Lamb & Harmon whom Raskob had hired two years earlier to design General Motors' new headquarters.

1930 marked the beginning of the fast and highly organized construction – using steel, concrete and bricks with limestone facing - of what would become the symbol of New York.

Twenties

Renowned for its honesty and its ability to meet deadlines, this studio took a new approach to this project, as Shreve said to a reporter: "Our plan is to find the finest brains in the construction field, in the various engineering specialties, architecture, construction and labor. Then we will put all our ideas on the table. And we will use the best of these ideas." On the other hand, in those years architecture as a profession was undergoing profound changes – and the architect's role was becoming that of designing profitable rather than esthetically pleasing buildings. Furthermore, when planning a construction project, especially skyscrapers it was becoming increasingly

Every day 3,000 men – skilled and unskilled – worked at the Empire State Building construction site.

Historical Notes

Design: Shreve, Lamb & Harmon Associates

Typology: building consists of nearly totally prefabricated parts

Foundation excavations started: 22 January 1930

Construction started: 17 March 1930

Construction rate: 4 stories per week

Brickwork completed: 13 November 1930

Total duration of work: 1 year and 45 days

Total man-hours: 7 million

Total cost: $40,948,900.

necessary to take engineering factors into account and to remain up-to-date on new materials and technologies. Construction was contracted out to Starrett Brothers and Eken, then considered the best in the field of skyscraper building. They deserve the credit for the efficient logistical organization that made it possible to put up the building in a record time of one year and 45 days, that is equal to 7 million man hours.

Demolition of the buildings that stood on the site of the new skyscraper began on 22 January 1930; the foundations were laid on 17 March of the same year and the building was completed in March 1931. Thus, the cost of erecting the Empire State Building was cut by 43 million dollars, thanks to the reduction in labor costs. The Empire State Building was opened on 1 May 1931, a cold, slightly misty day. At exactly 11:30 a.m. Al Smith's grandson cut the ribbon, while President Hoover turned on all the lights in the building from Washington. The opening mobilized everyone in New York who was anyone and the banquet that followed the ceremony was definitely the social highlight of the year. The 86th floor observation deck, the only one of the period was opened the following Sunday, with a record number of 5108 visitors. Initially, the Empire

"**L**ike little spiders they toiled, spinning a fabric of steel against the sky", *The New Yorker*.
An average of 3000 men, skilled and unskilled, worked at the Empire State Building construction site every day. Lewis Wickes Hines' famous pictures documenting the work can certainly be considered masterpieces of 20th century social photography.
The pictures of the welders' acrobatics as they nonchalantly hung in the air, hundreds of feet above ground to position and weld the steel beams have gone down in history.
In one week these welders assembled an average of 2400 tons of steel and managed to complete their contract in just six months.

Lewis Wickes Hines' photographs bear witness to the courage and daring of those men who worked at dizzying heights to build what is probably the world's most famous skyscraper.

Thirties

1931

1 May

The Empire State Building was officially opened at 11:15 a.m. on 1 May 1931; Al Smith presided over the ceremonies as his grandson cut the ribbon.

State Building was a greater success with tourists than in commercial terms. During the first year 775,000 visitors brought in $875,000 – that is 2% of the construction costs. Most of the office space, however, remained vacant for the first few years. In fact, after the euphoria of the Twenties the economy had already taken a downturn that developed into the Great Depression.

Notwithstanding the prestige of the address, that was underscored by an intensive advertising campaign, in 1936 only the first thirty floors had been rented. Not even the 1933 movie "King Kong" that made the Empire State Building famous throughout the world managed to boost the rents. Even though the economic situation was not rosy, the Empire State Building always looked impeccable. The 350 strong maintenance staff, included 200 cleaners, 8 window washers, a nurse and a team of fire fighters, on duty 24 hours a day. Alfred E. Smith played a crucial role in those years. It was he who welcomed the many famous visitors including Winston Churchill and Helen Keller and he attended every promotional event. And there is more: in 1932 it was his actions that helped reduce real estate taxes that had been estimated at 42 million dollars, revealing how little of the office space had actually been rented. The era of the skyscrapers had come to a halt and World War II was looming on the horizon.

Period Interiors

The same subdued elegance that characterizes the silhouette of the Empire State Building was to be found in the interiors that were designed by Rambush Studios, the same firm which, in the Twenties had designed more than 800 large movie theaters including the lavish Roxy Theater and later the lobby of the Waldorf Astoria and Radio City Music Hall. The walls of the two-story high lobby were faced with dark blue, yellow-veined marbled. The only decorative motif was a narrow frame that recalled those on

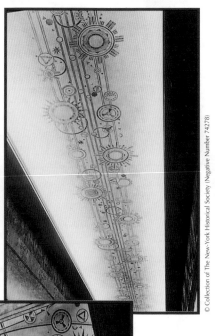

the exterior of the main entrance and stylized wings symbolizing the air-age. Behind the doorman's desk there is an enormous aluminum and marble mural of the building and the two main cities in New York State. The lamps that illuminate the lobby and hallways are concealed by frames and are directed upwards to cast light on the spectacular ceiling with its circle and star motif in

platinum, gold and aluminum leaf. To connect the mezzanine that is divided by two large entrances there are two chrome plated steel bridges decorated with linear patterns that evoke the motifs above the elevator doors.

The Offices

The offices were carefully designed by Shreve, Lamb & Harmon to maximize the amount of floor space receiving natural light and to offer versatile spaces that could be suited for small firms and large companies. Even though at the time the building was the finest example of the modern style, the tenants were quite conservative in their choice of office furnishings and preferred traditional styles. Wood paneled walls, neo-Renaissance furniture and even fireplaces characterized most of the management offices, such as John Raskob's Georgian rooms. The first truly modern office belonged to the 1939 New York World's Fair. The enormous conference room furnished with chrome chairs, neutral toned rugs and a huge shiny, linear table heralded a style that would become fashionable in the Fifties.

The Empire State Building's
second decade was marked
not only by World War II,
but also by a series of events that
were to be significant for its own
history. The outbreak of the war in
Europe had immediate effects in
America and especially New York,
the main North Atlantic seaport.
The upper, strategically positioned
floors were used as observatories
to sight the approach of enemy
aircraft. The eighty-sixth floor of
the Empire State Building was one

By the Forties Manhattan's skyline had been completely changed by the new skyscrapers that soared upwards, and the Empire State Building that stood out among them all.

of these points and some rooms on the eighty-first floor were converted into lounges for the lookouts so they could rest between shifts. After the attack on Pearl Harbor on 7 December 1941, the Empire State Building assigned five members of the staff to anti-aircraft surveillance, but the main problem was how to quickly evacuate the more than 8000 people who worked there every day. The stairwells and fire stairs in the middle of the building were designated as air raid shelters and every floor had a warden to coordinate emergency measures. The safety procedures inside the building were further improved with new equipment and all employees received a detailed instruction manual. Venetian blinds were put up on each window for

blackout purposes and the tower was also blacked out. Another consequence of the war was that a large portion of the staff was drafted, and was replaced by women.

Starting in April 1942 blackout rules were extended to more and more of the city, even the top of the Chrysler building was rendered less shiny and reflective.

Aside from the War, the Forties was a decade filled with events for the Empire State Building. First of all the increase in industrial output prompted by America's entry into the war caused a certain amount of economic recovery with positive effects on the construction market as well. In 1942 the first federal agency, the Office of Price Administration moved into the building.

1945: the Bomber

Among the many memorable and singular events that dot the Empire State Building's long history, we cannot forget what happened on 28 July 1945 when a U.S. Air Force B25 bomber crashed into the 79th story of the building because of heavy fog. The crash cost 14 people their lives, while an elevator operator who had dropped 79 stories in the cab miraculously survived thanks to the perfect workings of the emergency brakes. The building suffered severe damages which, however, did not compromise either its structural stability or statics.

1945

The OPA moved its regional headquarters to the Empire State Building and occupied five full floors. In 1946 85% of the building was leased: between private companies and federal agencies there were more than 85,000 people working there daily. These included the employees of the United Nations which had selected the Empire State Building as its temporary headquarters in 1946. By 1950 all the offices had finally been rented and the property was producing a gross income of 10 million dollars a year.

In the meantime, in September 1944 the building welcomed its five millionth visitor, the lucky tourist was a young RAF officer who was in New York for joint exercises with the American forces.

In 1945, just a few days before the end of the war a B25 bomber flying from Boston to Newark crashed between the seventy-eighth and seventy-ninth floors due to fog. The collision resulted in 14 deaths, 25 wounded and over one million dollars in total damage. This tragedy, however, confirmed the building's safety – the fire was tamed in 19 minutes and fully extinguished in 40 – and its structural stability.

In less than one month all the damages had been repaired and the fully restored Empire State Building entered what was to become its own "golden era".

1947: the Suicide Barrier

Given its height and fame, the Empire State Building has long exerted a particular draw for those who plan on taking their own lives. Since the beginning the building's managers took precautions to prevent dangerous situations, with close surveillance of the observatories. The first suicide from the Empire State Building however, took place even before it was completed when a worker who had lost his job at the construction site jumped from the seventy-second floor. The first suicide from the observation deck occurred in 1935.

Then, between 1935 and 1947 nine people jumped from the observation deck and six from various offices. In 1947 there were 2 suicides and five attempts. Therefore, the management decided to erect a new barrier. An 8 foot (2.5 meter) fence with a mesh wide enough to let a head, but not a body pass, topped by curved metal spikes facing inwards to prevent people from climbing over it was installed. Since then only 6 people have succeeded in killing themselves by leaping from the Empire State Building.

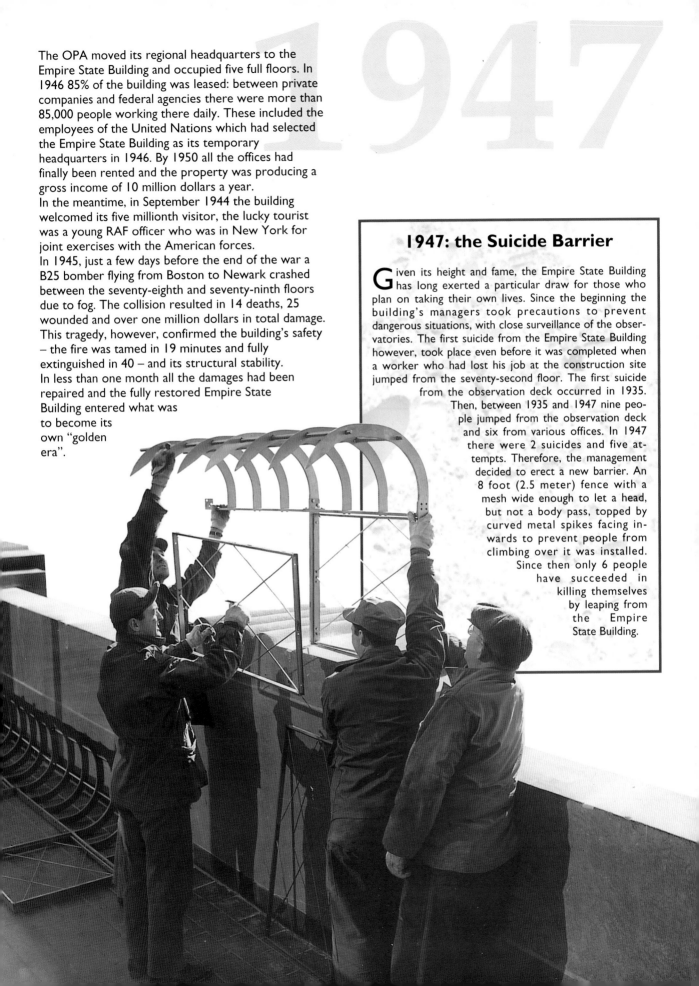

1950: Master Television Antenna

Since October 1930, months before its opening, the Empire State Building hosted the NBC radio antennas. In July 1931 NBC rented the eastern side of the 85th floor to build a station dedicated to experimental audio-video broadcasts. After the end of the World War II television began to replace radio as the most popular medium. In 1950 a 220 foot (67 meter) high television antenna was built, bringing the total height of the building to a new record of 1469.8 feet (448 meters). Even though the structure of the tower that was built as a mooring for dirigibles was certainly sturdy enough to hold the 60 tons of the antenna, it still had to be welded to the building's bearing structure. To minimize the work done on the outdoor scaffolding that was set up at over 1,312 feet (400 meters) above ground, with a base of slightly more than 18 square feet (2 square meters), all the prefabricated parts were assembled in the factory and hoisted on open-top elevators. The antenna was christened by William O'Dwyer, mayor of New York, in July 1950.

The Fifties were, for all intents and purposes, the golden era of the Empire State Building. All the floors were finally rented to even prestigious tenants such as the United Nations. The observatories were one of the compulsory stops, not only for tourists, but also for celebrities passing through New York like Sir Edmund Hillary, the finalists in the Miss World and Miss Universe contests and even Queen Elizabeth II – for whom the first and only red carpet was ever laid. John Raskob died in October 1950 and the building was put up for sale, the transaction was completed in December 1951 for a price of $51 million including more than one million to cover the fees of the lawyers and financial experts who had worked on the negotiations. The building was purchased by Realty Association Securities Corporation, a consortium of entrepreneurs from Detroit and Hollywood.

During this decade the life of the Empire State Building was also characterized by a series of technical improvements. Air conditioning was installed in 1951 and the loading zones around the building were expanded relieving traffic on the nearby streets. These innovations were not obvious to visitors or passers-by, however, the 220 foot (67 meter) high television antenna that was erected in 1950 certainly was. Broadcasts from the Empire State Building were not a novelty. The NBC radio and television network had been broadcasting from the top of the Empire State Building since 1931. For the building's owners, the growing popularity of TV was another significant source of income. With a new and powerful antenna signals from all the TV stations in the New York area could be clearly received in nearby cities and towns, bringing another $500,000 dollars annually to the Empire State Building.

Successful radio programs continued to be broadcast from the 86th floor such as "Tower to Tower" a Voice of America program that linked the world's four main radio and television towers: the Empire State Building in New York, the Eiffel Tower in Paris, the Berlin radio tower and the television tower in Stuttgart.

In 1954 ownership of the Empire State Building passed to Henry Crown who already had considerable investments in the Chicago real estate market and was a major shareholder of the Hilton Hotel chain. "The Freedom Lights" were installed in 1956, these were the world's most powerful beacons and measured nearly 7 feet (2 meters) in diameter each. The idea was to have the Empire State Building compete with the Statue of Liberty as the monument welcoming immigrants and visitors to the land of opportunity as more and more were arriving by air than by sea. During these years the Empire State Building became not only one of the world's most successful real estate operations, but also the most prestigious symbol of this great metropolis.

The Empire State Building in the Movies

Annie Hall (1977)
by Woody Allen, starring
Woody Allen and Diane Keaton
Daddy Long Legs (1955)
by Jean Negulesco, starring Fred
Astaire and Leslie Caron
Guys & Dolls (1955)
by Joseph Mankiewicz, starring
Marlon Brando and Jean Simmons
Independence Day (1996)
by Roland Emmerich, starring
Will Smith and Bill Pullman
King Kong (1933)
by Merian Cooper and E. Schedsak

Klute (1971)
by Alan Pakula starring
Jane Fonda and Donald Sutherland
Last Action Hero (1993)
by John McTiernan, starring
Arnold Schwarzenegger and
A. Murray Abraham
New York, New York (1977)
by Martin Scorsese, starring
Liza Minelli and Robert De Niro
On the Waterfront (1954)
by Elia Kazan starring
Marlon Brando and Karl Malden
The Pawnbroker (1965)
by Sidney Lumet
starring Rod Steiger and
Geraldine Fitzgerald
Shaft (1971)
by Gordon Parks, starring
Richard Roundtree, Moses Gum

Sleepless in Seattle (1993)
by Nora Ephrom, starring Meg Ryan
and Tom Hanks
Superman II (1980)
by Richard Lester, starring
Gene Hackman, Christopher Reeve
Taxi Driver (1976)
by Martin Scorsese, starring
Robert De Niro and Jodie Foster
When Harry Met Sally (1986)
by Rob Reiner, starring Meg Ryan
and Billy Crystal

*A scene from the 1954 episode
(Lucy Is Envious) of **I Love Lucy** with
Lucy and Ethel pretending
to be aliens who land
on the Empire State Building.*

Fifties

*For the 50th anniversary of the **1933** film **King Kong**, an inflatable, eight-story tall, vinyl gorilla that was visible throughout the city was perched on the Empire State Building.*

Curiosities

The life of the Empire State Building is filled with curious and sometimes downright bizarre facts and events. One of these is the "Empire State Building Race", the annual race in which the contestants have to run up the stairs to the 102nd floor...as fast as they can.

One decidedly romantic rendezvous is Valentine's Day, couples can marry in the Empire State Building and thus become members of the Empire State Wedding Club.

On the subject of romance, kissing at the top of this building can be a truly electrifying experience under certain weather conditions. Barely touching lips will set

Famous Visitors

Ever since its opening the Empire State Building is a "must" for all the celebrities who come to New York: kings and heads of state, Hollywood stars, including Lassie and circus stars. Until 1944 it was Al Smith who acted as official host to people such as Winston Churchill, Alice Hargreaves Liddel (the inspiration behind *Alice in Wonderland*) and even Sitting Bull, Jr., who traded Al Smith his derby for a feather headdress. The only celebrity who refused to go to the top of the Empire State Building was Fay Wray, the star of the 1933 film, King Kong. No one knows whether her acrophobia was real or merely a publicity stunt, but it certainly did contribute to drawing crowds to the movie theaters. Another famous visitor was the aviator Douglas Corrigan who, in 1938, took off on a solo flight from New York to Los Angeles and landed in Dublin. When he was asked to point out the Newark airport from the observation deck, Corrigan pointed straight to the Queensborough Bridge, confirming his reputation to the general hilarity.

*In October 1957 on the occasion of the state visit of **Queen Elizabeth II**, right center, and **Prince Philip**, a red carpet was laid in the Empire State Building for the first and only time.*

off tiny electric shocks caused by the enormous accumulation of static electricity.

And finally, if the view from the observation deck wants to make you fly, you can see the tops of all New York's skyscrapers close-up by taking the simulated 3-D flight on the first floor.

*1983: **the winner** of the **Empire State Building Race** crossing the finish line. The race up the 1860 steps to the top of the Empire State Building is held every year. The contestants are many, well-trained and fierce. The current record is 9'53".*

Following pages: the contours of the Empire State Building stand out against the sky at sunset.

*Since 1963 there are **eight full color panels** in the lobby of the Empire State Building. They were made by the artists Roy Sarkia and Renée Nemerov using different techniques. These panels depict the seven wonders of the ancient world: Great pyramid of Cheops – 481 feet; the Hanging Gardens of Babylon – 30 ft; Statue of Zeus – 49 ft; Temple of Diana over 50 ft; Lighthouse of Pharos – 600 ft; Colossus of Rhodes – 160 ft; Tomb of King Mausolus) flanked by the Empire State Building as the eight wonder of the modern world.*

Souvenirs

The Empire State Building has always been a mecca for souvenir collectors. The first ever sold were the classic paperweights, letter openers and postcards with the words or pictures of the Empire State Building. Some of the postcards with exclusive views in an elegant black and silver box designed by Brooks & Porter are highly sought after. Another choice collector's piece is the box of chocolates created by the pastry chef J. B. Black for the opening.

In 1938 the souvenir shop located on the 86th floor observation deck began selling miniatures and lamps with bases shaped like the building, but the most valuable souvenir was certainly the one given to Queen Elizabeth II during her visit: a gold plated miniature of the Empire State Building with a ruby for the beacon made by Tiffany.

Skyscrapers

The Giants of New York

FLATIRON
(Fuller Building)
1902 *(285 ft/87 meters)*
WOOLWORTH BUILDING
1913 *(782 ft/241 meters)*
CHRYSLER BUILDING
1930 *(1130 ft/319 meters)*
EMPIRE STATE BUILDING
1931 *(1247 ft/381 meters)*
GE BUILDING
(Rockefeller Center)
1940 *(850 ft/259 meters)*
METLIFE BUILDING
1963 *(801 ft/246 meters)*
TWIN TOWERS
1972-73
(1379 ft/417 –1362 ft/415 meters)
TRUMP TOWER
1983 *(657 ft/202.5)*

More than one hundred years have passed since the construction of the first skyscraper, but the New York panorama continues to change and change. The passions aroused by these towers that seem to touch the sky has not diminished. Different generations of architects have tested themselves against this type of building applying new architectural styles, creating daring structures, using new materials and proposing original solutions. New York is a city that is built upwards. Walking along the streets amidst these still concrete giants can be an intimidating experience because seen from the sidewalk their bulk seems inhuman and sometimes it is even difficult to see the tops. However, it is sufficient to change perspective and go up to the observatories to enjoy a fascinating view that will let you appreciate the talent and commitment that made these structures possible. It is impossible to forget that behind each of these giants there are always people, and looking at their creations we can perceive the dreams, ambitions, will and skill that made it possible for humans to fulfill this magnificent dream.

*Below: **Lower Manhattan**, where the **East River** and the **Hudson River** meet at the harbor; on pages 48-49 an aerial view of Manhattan's skyscrapers at twilight.*

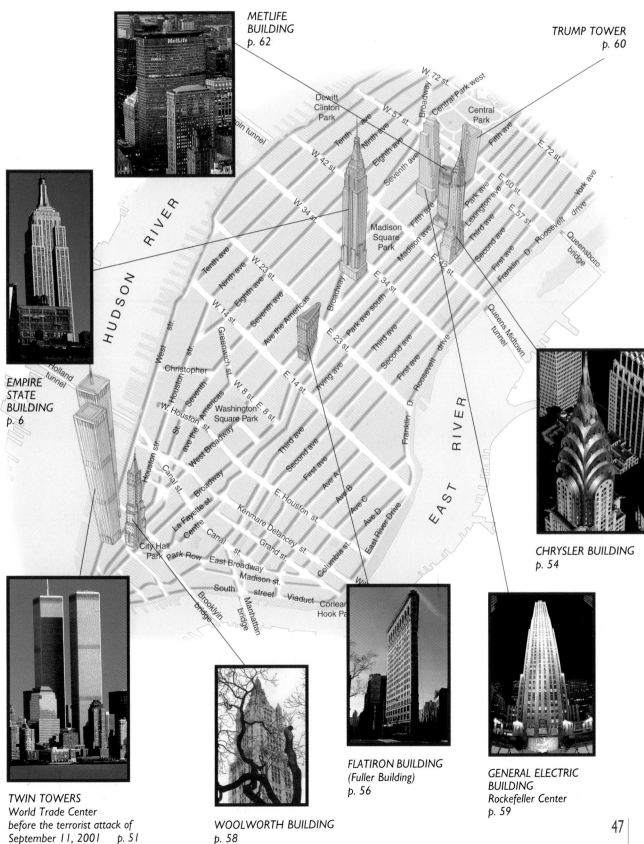

METLIFE BUILDING
p. 62

TRUMP TOWER
p. 60

EMPIRE STATE BUILDING
p. 6

CHRYSLER BUILDING
p. 54

TWIN TOWERS
World Trade Center before the terrorist attack of September 11, 2001   p. 51

WOOLWORTH BUILDING
p. 58

FLATIRON BUILDING
(Fuller Building)
p. 56

GENERAL ELECTRIC BUILDING
Rockefeller Center
p. 59

Twin Towers

The impressive Twin Towers, at the southern tip of Manahattan Island between Vesey and Liberty Streets and West and Church Streets, were one of the world's largest business complexes: the World Trade Center. The idea developed in the early 1960's as part of a plan to relaunch the downtown area as an international business and financial center; in fact, the New York Stock Exchange was also originally slated to move there.

The backers reviewed hundreds of plan before they selected Minoru Yamasaki and Emery Roth as architects; actual construction work began in 1969. The Towers were built of 181,000 tons of steel; the parts were prefabricated in the Midwest US and lifted into place by eight specially-built cranes brought in from Australia. The towers of the World Trade Center opened on April 4, 1973. The 1 WTC tower soared to a height of 1709 feet (521 m) with its television antenna; its twin, 2 WTC to 1362 feet (415 m). Both stood on foundations sunk to a depth of 755 feet (23 m). Although the towers were not very interesting from a stylistic standpoint, they opened equipped with a state-of-the-art telecommunications

The Winter Garden

Before the disaster of September 11, 2001, the spectacular Winter Garden in the World Financial Center, adjacent to the World Trade Center, was linked to it by an elegant covered elevated passageway. The view of the Hudson River and Ellis Island from this glass and steel building was magnificent. Its high nave hosted a palm grove that served as a garden setting for the cafes, restaurants, and bookstores that surrounded it, while the unconventional semicircular staircase in red and grey marble was used as an amphitheater for many events staged in this fascinating corner of New York.

The two parallel piped towers of steel and glass that were the Twin Towers soared heavenward over the lower tip of Manhattan and for years were an essential feature of the city skyline.

system comprising the first fiberoptic audiovisual network for commercial use ever installed in the United States. The observatory on the top floor of 1 WTC offered the city's most intoxicating view of New York and the Hudson River, with Staten Island, Ellis Island, and the Statue of Liberty. The famous "Windows on the World" restaurant and cocktail lounge—one of the city's most elegant spots—was located on the 107th floor.

Chrysler Building

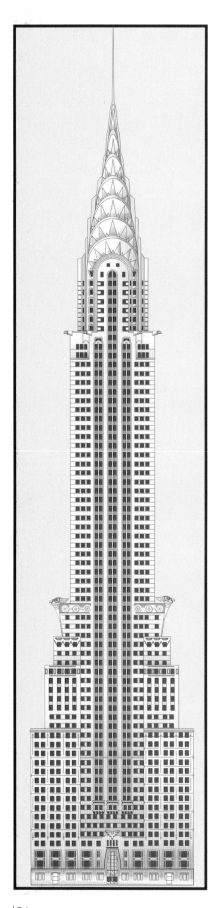

The steel spire and distinctive architecture make the Chrysler Building one of the city's symbols.

The Chrysler building is certainly one of the world's most recognizable skyscrapers with its steel Art Déco crown. Constructed in 1930 this 77 story building is located at 405 Lexington Avenue at 42nd Street and soars to a height 1130 feet (319 meters). The project was initially started by former senator William J. Reynolds and was then taken over by Walter P. Chrysler of the automobile company. Like many magnates of the period who got involved in this type of project, Walter Chrysler was essentially motivated by the prestige that the tallest building in the world would confer on his name and business. The design by the New York architect William Van Alen was therefore modified several times so that Chrysler could obtain this record. Shortly before work was completed, Van Alen played his trump card and a 184 feet (56 meter) tall spire that had been constructed in great secrecy in the yard was hoisted above the cupola in 90 minutes. It was, however, a short-lived victory since the record was broken by the Empire State Building just a few months later.

The striking steel cupola by Nirosta is certainly the most fascinating element of this building. The stainless steel facing was arranged in rays with numerous triangular windows that follow the seven concentric parabolic curves on the four sides of the cupola.

The building's façades are much less original with black, white and grey oriental style motifs. On Chrysler's request Van Alen added decorations that symbolize the automaker such as stylized cars and another inspired by wheel rims, while the recesses on the upper floors were embellished with steel eagles whose wings are the logo of the company, and a few mock spouts in Gothic style. Unfortunately these ornamental motifs are barely visible from street level, and even the base and entrance to the building can readily pass unobserved. The interiors, however, are extraordinary and have been restored to their original glory by the restructuring work done by the new proprietors in 1999. The entrance walls are faced with sumptuous red Moroccan marble, while the floor is made of yellow Siena marble with an amber

William Van Alen

William Van Alen (1893-1954) began studying architecture at the Pratt Institute in Brooklyn, where he was born. In 1908 he won a scholarship that allowed him to attend the École des Beaux Arts in Paris. He returned to New York in 1911 where he opened a studio with H. Craig Severance.

Soon the two made a name for themselves with their innovative styles, especially in multi-story commercial buildings.

In 1925 Van Alen struck out on his own and four years later began working on the plans for the Chrysler Building. Even though this building is one of the masterpieces of Art Déco architecture, when the work was finally completed Walter Chrysler refused to pay him, accusing him of fraud and collusion with some contractors.

The architect appealed, but the suit was soon dropped. Even today, no one knows whether he was ever paid. Van Alen continued working, but because of the accusations launched by his client coupled with the Great Depression, he never had another opportunity to work on a project as prestigious as the Chrysler Building.

In 1930 the Chrysler Building broke the height record held by the Woolworth Building, but not even one year later a new record was made by the Empire State Building that became the protagonist of the New York panorama.

and blue frame. The ceiling is covered with an enormous mural by Edward Turnbull entitled "Energy, result, workmanship and transportation."

Other noteworthy points are the elevators: the fine, carved wooden doors are considered Art Déco masterpieces. The staircase, with the magnificent chromed-plated balustrade leading to the mezzanine and basement is also made in the same style. The observation deck below the spire is another spectacular portion of the Chrysler building, with its triangular windows that are tilted inwards. Unfortunately the observatory has been closed to the public for years.

Flatiron Building

In 1903 the 285 feet (87 meters) of the Flatiron Building, at 23rd Street, where Fifth Avenue crosses Broadway, made it the tallest building.

Even though it was never the tallest skyscraper in the world, the Flatiron Building is certainly one of the most original and most photographed buildings in the world. Its triangular shape and location at the intersection of Fifth Avenue and Broadway at 23rd Street is one of the symbols of the city. Built in 1902 as the headquarters of the Fuller Construction Company, it rises 285 feet (87 meters) and is considered New York's oldest skyscraper. Originally it was known as the "Fuller Building", but the people constantly called it "Flatiron" so the nickname became the official name.
The plans were prepared by Daniel H. Burnham who had already achieved a certain amount of fame for other skyscrapers in Chicago.
From the engineering standpoint, the building immediately stood out as one of the most modern in New York since it had an independent electric heating system. For the exterior Burnham

drew his inspiration from the Italian Renaissance. The idea was to make it resemble a very tall classic column with a capital through plays of perspective. Therefore, it was built according to traditional architectural canons with a ground floor of shops, developing on the central stories and a conclusion with an elaborate cornice above the 21st story.

Daniel Hudson Burnham

Daniel H. Burnham (1846-1912) is considered one of the major architects and city planners in America at the turn of the 19th century. Today, four of the skyscrapers he designed on his own (the Flatiron, New York) or with his partner John Wellbron Root (the Rookery, the Reliance Building and the Monadnock Building in Chicago) are national landmarks. The urban layout of Chicago in the last decade of the 19th century, considered to be thirty years ahead of its time, was widely imitated in other large American cities.

As opposed to other architects of the era, Burnham did not study at any prestigious European art school: after he finished his secondary education he went to work as an apprentice for the architects Carter, Drake and Wight. In 1873 he left to open a studio with Root, and soon specialized in steel skyscrapers. In 1881, the year his partner died, he was awarded the contract to design the World Columbian Exposition of 1893 that laid the foundations, as it were for Chicago's urban development. The other famous buildings he designed include Selfridges's Department store in London (1909) and Union Station in Washington D.C. (1909).

Actually, Burnham succeeded so well that at first New Yorkers refused to visit the building because they were afraid it would fall over because of the strong winds at that intersection. But, if the gusts of wind never made it fall, they did contribute to its popularity.

Hordes of men would stand around the apex of the building hoping to catch of glimpse of ankles as the wind raised the skirts of the ladies who strolled by.

Woolworth Building

The 1913 Neo-Gothic Woolworth Building, was the tallest building ever erected, and it held the record until 1930.

Considered by many to be the most beautiful commercial building in the world – it was nicknamed the "cathedral of commerce", this skyscraper, designed by the architect Cass Gilbert is, in fact a masterpiece of the Neo-Gothic style that was in vogue in the United States at the beginning of the 20th century. Erected in 1913 at 223 Broadway, the Woolworth Building that reaches to a height of 729 feet maintained its primacy as the world's tallest until 1930. Frank Woolworth, founder of the famous chain store paid 13.5 million dollars in cash, thus launching a race among the magnates of the period that would continue throughout the Twenties. The building comprises a 27 story body and a 60 story tower on Broadway. Gargoyles, arches and swirls follow each other on the façades that were restored to their original splendor in 1980 – the restoration work cost more than construction! If the opulence of the exterior does not fail to arouse the admiration and wonder of anyone passing nearby, the interior is no less striking. The lobby is definitely one of the most lavish and elegant in New York. The vaulted ceilings are clad with mosaics as brilliant and sparkling as jewels and intricate, yet delicate wrought iron and bronze ornaments abound.

The lobby is also decorated with bronze sculptures, one of which portrays Frank Woolworth counting the "nickels and dimes" on which he built his fortune.

The Nickel n'Dime Empire

Born in 1852 at Rodman New York, Frank Winfield Woolworth is the classic example of the self-made man who built an immense fortune out of nothing in the New World. Son of poor farmers, at his death Woolworth left a personal fortune of 65 million dollars. He began his career as a stock-boy in a store when he was twenty.

In 1879 after having heard about the success of selling items priced at 5 cents from a peddler, he convinced his employer to lend him a little less than $400 to open the first store where everything cost one nickel (5 cents).

The beginning was not easy, but Woolworth did not give up and in the end he managed to find the right places and products for his stores. Business took off after the recession of 1893 and Woolworth began opening his stores in the big cities such as Washington, Boston and Philadelphia. His dreams were crowned by the opening of a large store in Manhattan in 1896 where there was even an organ. In 1897 he contacted the architect Cass Gilbert to build his corporate headquarters downtown. When Gilbert asked him how tall the building should be he answered "750 feet." "You mean that is my limit," asked the architect to which the magnate replied, "No, that is the minimum."

World War I caused Woolworth some problems since he imported much merchandise from Europe, but it did not stop the growth of his chain that reached as far as Great Britain.

Woolworth died in 1919 of a tooth infection that he stubbornly refused to have treated.

GE Building

Originally known as the RCA (Radio Corporation of America) Building, the General Electric Building with its 850 feet (259 meters) is the tallest edifice in Rockefeller Center. Completed in 1933 this Art Déco structure is the culmination of several lessons learned during the construction of the Empire State Building which it does not resemble even in the slightest. First of all the façade is made of Indiana limestone and its vertical sweep is achieved by the alignment of the windows. Even the interior was designed so that natural light could reach all the leasable floor space, maximizing its value. But even if the exterior is not particularly interesting, extreme care went into the design of the interior. The Art Déco ornamentation was inspired by classical mythology and the Rockefellers used the services of a philosopher to conceptualize the decorative theme. In the niche above the main entrance is the famous relief sculpture "Genius" by Lee Lawrie, while the walls are covered with murals by José Mari Sert.

Radio City Music Hall

Rockefeller Center is the home of Radio City Music Hall, an institution in the New York world of entertainment. Since 1936, the year it was opened, to today over 300 million people have attended shows in this 6,200 seat theater that is still the largest and best equipped indoor theater anywhere in the world. The "Christmas Spectacular" show featuring the Rockettes is certainly the most famous, but even the rest of the calendar is filled with prestigious and high quality events. Part of the theater's long lived success is due to the fabulous American Art Déco interior that ever since the beginning aroused such a sensation that one critic wrote, "It has been said of the new Music Hall that it needs no performers."
The designer Donald Desky, following the general theme "Human Achievement" created a tribute to the successes of the human race in the fields of the arts, sciences and industry. All the interiors are original pieces made by Desky or artisans he hired using both traditional precious (gold leaf and marble) and industrial (bakelite, permatex and aluminum) materials.

*The 850 foot (259 meters) Art Déco
GE Building in the middle of Rockefeller Center.*

Opposite the building is the large, sunken Rockefeller Plaza that has been a luxurious ice skating rink since 1936 in winter and an elegant outdoor café in summer. The bronze statue of Prometheus by Paul Manship adorns the large fountain.

Trump Tower

Completed in 1983, the Trump Tower is located at 725 Fifth Avenue in the most elegant part of Midtown Manhattan; it is named for the builder and owner, Donald Trump. Designed by the architect Der Scurr, of Swanke, Hayden, Connel & Co., this 68 story skyscraper (657 feet – 202 meters) is one of the most interesting examples of the first phase of the postmodern style. The classic parallelepiped with dark glass windows is enlivened by a diagonal cut on the corner of 5th Avenue and 56th Street. On that side the building rises with vertical and horizontal terraces that are decorated with ornamental plants. This is truly a multipurpose skyscraper: between the ground and sixth floors there are stores and restaurants, between the 7th and 20th are offices, while the remaining forty stories are home to 266 luxury apartments that are leased to tenants such as Sophia Loren and Johnny Carson. The lobby is lavishly decorated with red marble, mirrors and shining brass in the opulent style of the Eighties. The main attraction is definitely the five-story high waterfall that dominates the main entrance of the shopping area.

Symbol of the yuppie generation and the extravagance of the Eighties, Donald Trump constructed this building that has a five-story waterfall in the main lobby.

Donald Trump and His Empire

A true New Yorker from Queens, Donald Trump was certainly the most famous developer in the United States in the Eighties and Nineties thanks to a series of lucky deals and his passion for beautiful women. His first big real estate deal dates from 1976 when he purchased the neglected Commodore Hotel next to Grand Central Station and transformed it into the elegant – and profitable hotel.

The **Trump Tower** where he maintains his offices and home – a 53 room penthouse – is his second prestigious undertaking. Between the Eighties and Nineties the Trump empire was growing at dizzying speeds, and not only in the field of luxury real estate in New York, Atlantic City, the Las Vegas of the East Coast, but it also expanded to sports (he bought a New Jersey football team), an airline, a modeling agency and a construction company. At the beginning of the Nineties the recession put a stop to this growth and Trump was forced to relinquish some prestigious properties such as the Plaza Hotel in New York.

In 1997 he completed the **Trump International Hotel & Tower**, a luxurious hotel and commercial building next to Central Park, while his most recent project is the Trump World tower, the world's tallest residential building.

MetLife Building

The octagonal base of the MetLife Building resembles the wing of a plane, most suitable for Pan American Airlines, the original owners who occupied it until 1981.

The MetLife Building, originally known as the Pan Am Building is one of New York's most controversial skyscrapers. Its bulk not only breaks the view of Park Avenue, the most elegant street in Manhattan, but it also blocks the classic beauty of Grand Central Terminal. Notwithstanding these criticisms, this 1963 building located at 200 Park Avenue at 45th Street is one of the city's finest examples of the International Style. The project was originally awarded to Emery Roth who was joined by Walter Gropius and Pietro Belluschi as consultants. Gropius raised the height to 59 stories 807 feet (246 meters) and conceived an octagonal base so that the building resembled the wing of an airplane, perfect for the main tenant, Pan American Airlines. The glass, cement and granite façade is enlivened by two colonnades at the 21st and 46th floors, while the lobby is decorated with artworks such as the mural by Joseph Albers and the metal cable installation entitled "Flight" by Richard Lippol.

The MetLife Building, an outstanding example of the International Style has caused a great outcry from the day it was built in 1963 because it obstructs the view of Park Avenue.

The lobby is connected to the railroad terminal by a series of covered passages.
In 1981 Pan Am sold the building to the MetLife insurance company that changed its name.

Grand Central Terminal

Grand Central Terminal is unique in the world, from both the architectural and social standpoints. Not only is it unanimously considered a masterpiece of American architecture, but every day over 400,000 people go through it, creating a fascinating weave of lives and events. Built between 1903 and 1913 Grand Central Terminal is a combination of Beaux Arts Eclecticism of grandiose yet elegant and harmonious proportions with innovative engineering that makes it possible handle the enormous daily flow of passenger and train traffic. The main lobby and ticket office never cease to astound anyone who has seen Paul Helleu's fresco of the constellations that shines down from the vaulted ceiling. A recent restructuring project resulted in the creation of a lively mall with luxury boutiques and a huge variety of fast-food stores between the ground floor and underground level.

Bibliography

American History, March 1998, "The Nickel'n Dime Empire" by Gustaitis, Joseph

Biography, June 1998, "Donald Trump in Trump: the Art of the Deal" by Wohl, Alexander

Goldman, Jonathan, "The Empire State Building Book", St. Martin's Press, 1980

Lopate, Philip ed., "Writing New York: a literary anthology", The Library of America, 1998

Tauranac, John, "The Empire State Building: the making of a Landmark", St. Martin's Griffin, New York, 1997

Wolfe, Gerard R., "New York, a guide to the metropolis", McGraw-Hill, 1994

INDEX

© Copyright by Casa Editrice Bonechi - Florence - Italy
Fax +39 0555000766
E-mail: bonechi@bonechi.it - Internet: www.bonechi.it - www.bonechi.com

Publication created by Casa Editrice Bonechi
Publication manager: Monica Bonechi
Photographic research by the Editorial Staff of the Casa Editrice Bonechi
Graphic design, layout and cover: Manuela Ranfagni
Editing: Giovannella Masini

Text: Maria Elena Velardi
Translation: Julia Weiss

Pages 51,52: translation by Paula Boomsliter
Drawings pages 8, 12, 13, 47, 54 by Stefano Benini
Map on page 6 by Daniela Mariani

Printed in Italy by
Centro Stampa Editoriale Bonechi.

ISBN 88-476-0895-3

* * *

PHOTOGRAPHY ACKNOWLEDGMENTS

AP/Wide World Photos:
pages 38; 39; 40 (John Carucci); 42 above (Ron Frehm); 42 below; 43 above (David Pickoff).
Avery Architectural and Fine Arts Library, Columbia University in the City of New York:
pages 25 right; 33 above left and below; 34 above left; 41.
Battman Studios:
pages 3; 4-5; 14 above and below; 18-19; 20; 21; 44-45; 48-49; 57 right center.
© Bedford/Downing (Igor Maloratsky Ph.):
pages 56 center (#800); right (#806); 58 left (#901).
Library of Congress, reproduced from the collections of the:
page 32.
Museum of the City of New York:
pages 14 center; 16.
Romana Javitz Collection. Miriam and Ira D. Wallach Division of Art, Prints & Photographs. The New York Public Library:
pages 28 above, right and left; 30; 31.
Alan Schein/NYC:
pages 22; 23; 50; 52 above and below left; 53; 56 above; 57 above and below left; 60.
© Collection of The New-York Historical Society:
pages 9 small photograph; 13 center; 26 below; 27; 28 below; 29; 34 below left; 34 right, above and below; 35; 43 below.

Photographs from the Archives of Casa Editrice Bonechi, taken by:
Andrea Pistolesi: pages 2; 6; 7; 8; 9 large photograph; 10-11; 15; 17 large photograph; 46; 51; 54; 55; 58; 59; 62; 63.
Paolo Giambone: pages 17 small photograph; 33 small photograph on the right; 61.

Cover photo: Andrea Pistolesi.

The publisher apologizes for any unintentional omissions. We would be pleased to include any appropriate acknowledgments of which we are informed in subsequent editions of this publication.